ACCESS
WITHOUT VISA

Reaching people that other methods do
not reach

Eileen Bannister

WEC PUBLICATIONS
GERRARDS CROSS

First published 1995

ISBN 0 900828 73 0

British Library Cataloguing-in-Publication Data. A
catalogue record for this book is available from the British
Library.

Jointly published by
WEC PUBLICATIONS
Bulstrode, Oxford Road,
Gerrards Cross, Bucks. SL9 8SZ
and
SOON
Vere Lodge, 44 Twyford Road,
Willington, Derby, DE65 6BN

Cover designed by John Tromans

Typeset, printed and bound by
WEC Press, Gerrards Cross, Bucks. SL9 8SZ

CONTENTS

Fred and Lois Chapman at work on Bientôt

Chapter One

GAINING ATTENTION

"I sentence you to three years in prison." Tankoh's blood ran cold as he listened to the judgment. His life was already in a mess as a result of smoking Indian hemp and excessive drinking. Now he faced three years!

Brought up in Nigeria, Tankoh Jibril had been taught the truths of Christianity. Despite reading the Bible, however, bad habits clung to him, and try as he might he could not release himself.

Detention only added to his misery. A meagre supply of drugs found its way to the inmates via illicit channels and ugly scenes often resulted. Tankoh wondered if things would ever be any different.

One day a prison officer handed him a paper headed *SOON!*. Written in easy English, Tankoh found he could understand it without much difficulty. An article entitled 'I Fight Them' caught his eye. It told of a young man from Ghana who could not sleep due to evil spirits. Night after night they tormented him until he was in utter despair. He tried various 'remedies': drugs, night clubs and other activities, but they brought no relief. Then a friend told him about some special healing meetings. Out of curiosity he went along. There he heard what Jesus Christ could do for him. Asking God's forgiveness, he was delivered from sin and from the evil spirits that had oppressed him. That night Kwabena slept soundly, a free man at last!

This testimony made a deep impression on Tankoh Jibril. What he needed was power to overcome his evil habits. He decided to speak to God just as Kwabena had done. Tears mingled with remorse as he poured out his heart. Despite his wrongdoing, God loved him and would forgive him. In the days that followed Tankoh found he could say 'No' to the drink and drugs that had enslaved him. There in the confines of that Nigerian prison, he discovered a new purpose in life.

The chain of events that resulted in Tankoh's transformation began thousands of miles away in Derby, England. Many months previously John Lewis had been poring over a pile of articles that lay on his desk, searching for suitable items for the next issue of *SOON!* He thought of the terrible darkness which encompassed many throughout the world because of demonic influences. Suddenly his eyes alighted on the story of Kwabena Darko. "That's just what people need to know," he exclaimed. God had worked for Kwabena. He could do the same for others.

Thirty years earlier John had become aware of the desperate shortage of suitable gospel literature in the developing nations. As deputation secretary for the Worldwide Evangelisation Crusade, or WEC International as it is now called, John met many missionaries on furlough. Frequently they expressed the need for effective Christian literature. Attractive, well-produced communist literature they saw in abundance, even in African villages. What they had did not compare.

In his work John travelled widely. The long train journeys gave him time to indulge his favourite pastime of reading. On the way to one meeting, he was studying Dr Frank Laubach's book *Towards World Literacy*. The author advocated the use of simple English to reach the masses to whom English was a second language, stressing the need for simplicity in both method and materials. Dr Laubach's conviction, "If someone can produce something in easy English, they would gain the attention of the world", was shared by John. That something, John believed, should be a gospel broadsheet.

The concept of a gospel broadsheet had been developed by Fred and Lois Chapman, WEC missionaries from Africa. After twenty-three years working in the Ivory Coast, they moved to the then Belgian Congo to help with a Christian magazine called *Envol*. However, they soon discovered there were disadvantages with a magazine that was obtained by subscription. In poverty-stricken Africa it was simply too expensive for the majority of the people. Readers would only buy it if it contained items they liked, not necessarily those they needed.

Fred and Lois returned to the UK convinced that there must be a better way. In time the Lord showed Fred that a single-page newspaper containing relevant testimonies could be produced comparatively cheaply and easily. Distribution by international mail would enable thousands to be contacted if it were free of charge.

At a meeting organised by John Lewis in 1959 Fred shared his vision for a free gospel broadsheet, and the response far exceeded his expectations. Mr Fleming from Wright's (printers) of Sandbach, Cheshire, offered to print the broadsheet and then presented him with a gift to launch the paper. Suddenly his God-given dream was becoming a reality.

As Fred and Lois contemplated this new venture, they read the last chapter of the Bible, Revelation 22, where three times the Lord Jesus Christ says, "I am coming soon." The word in French which seemed to stand out was *bientôt,* meaning 'soon'. So they adopted this as the name of the paper. The emphasis was to be on the second coming of Christ. At the WEC headquarters the possibility of launching such a paper was still being considered when Fred strode into the room and pinned the first copy of *Bientôt* on the notice board!

In the cramped surroundings of their attic bedroom on the third floor of the old WEC Headquarters in Upper Norwood, London, Fred and Lois packed and addressed the broadsheets. Getting into bed often involved careful manoeuvres to avoid stepping on the piles of literature! With the help of candidates and staff the first issue of 10,000 copies was quickly despatched.

Demand grew rapidly as missionaries and others wrote in saying, "This is what we have been waiting for. Please send more copies." So each issue more were printed. Some questioned the wisdom of such a ministry. "What if it increased to such an extent that thousands of pounds would be required to finance it?" Undaunted, Fred knew he could trust God, just as George Müller and others before him had done. God honoured his faith, and as the number of copies increased, so did the supply.

In May-June 1961 leaders from the WEC Mission around the world gathered for a month's meetings at Kilcreggan in Scotland to explore God's way forward. Amongst other matters, the success of the gospel broadsheet *Bientôt* was recognised. The vision for similar broadsheets in other languages was embraced as part of a strategy to accomplish the evangelisation of the world and hasten Christ's return.

During the next few months, God confirmed to John Lewis that he should start a broadsheet in English and to

Leslie Brierley, a former WEC missionary to Portuguese West Africa, that he should produce a broadsheet in Portuguese called *Cedo*. These formed the start of the family of WEC gospel broadsheets now called 'Gospel Literature Worldwide'. Replacements in the form of Jack and Peggy Aitken released John and his wife Nellie from their responsibilities at WEC Headquarters for their new assignment.

John realised that a paper of this nature could help the millions who were eager to learn English, and also serve as an introduction to a new way of life through Jesus Christ. From the outset, John adopted some of the same principles of communication used in *Bientôt*, but he also incorporated ideas on methods of effective communication expressed in Dr Laubach's book *Towards World Literacy* and in *Message and Mission* by Dr Eugene Nida of the American Bible Society. The English version, called *SOON!* after the French one, should declare all essentials of the gospel message in a meaningful way through a reduced vocabulary of 1,500 widely-known English words.

This raised the question of how fundamental Christian concepts could be conveyed. What do words such as 'sin', 'repentance' and 'prayer' mean to a Hindu, Buddhist or even an atheist? If understood at all, they can have quite different meanings from what is intended in the Bible. So John decided to use simple words and phrases such as 'wrongdoing', 'a selfish spirit', 'a changed life' and 'speaking to God'.

Armed with the Laubach word list which included all words in most common use, plus a thesaurus, John set about rewriting appropriate testimonies and articles from Christian periodicals which would furnish a store of potential material for the broadsheet. He decided the emphasis should be on true-life stories from people of various nationalities.

Using eye-catching headlines to gain attention, he focused on the needs of which people were actually aware, just as Jesus had done when He spoke to the woman at the well. The Christian message must be seen to be relevant to the needs of which people are conscious. In addition, man's curiosity regarding future events and his desire to know how other people live were both factors which governed the nature of its contents. John also decided to include articles examining contemporary issues from a Biblical standpoint.

Aware that many people find it difficult or impossible to write letters, John saw that an essential element of the broadsheet should be a coupon. This way, people could easily write in for free follow-up material in the form of a Bible course. Finally, in March 1962, the first issue of 10,000 copies of *SOON!* was printed and despatched.

The fact that everything *SOON!* offered was free attracted recipients, particularly in the Third World. This policy has not been without its critics. Such offers may produce a high response, but this does not necessarily indicate that everyone who writes in is concerned for their spiritual wellbeing. However, if one soul is saved for every 100 or 1,000 broadsheets sent out, who can argue that it is not worth the effort?

Letters began arriving regularly at the SOON office which confirmed this. Noah, a young Nigerian, came from a Christian family but did not know the Lord himself. While visiting Bombay to purchase items for his shop back home, he bought some heroin for his own use. When he changed planes in France on his return journey he was arrested, tried and convicted. During his term in the French prison, he was given a copy of *SOON!* and later he sent for a correspondence course. On the very day it arrived, he accepted Jesus as his Saviour. For the remainder of his sentence he shared with other inmates the joy that Christ had brought to him and once a week led a group of ten in a Bible study.

Now it is one thing to print 10,000 broadsheets. Sending them free of charge to thousands of people worldwide is another matter. How could the broadsheet be posted to a large number of individuals, and where would one find their addresses? This method of distribution had been chosen because people in the Third World who receive direct mail from a foreign country acquire a certain amount of prestige.

Initially, John concentrated on finding addresses in the countries of the former British empire. One of the first methods of obtaining addresses was to copy them from overseas telephone directories which could be consulted at the Guildhall Library in London. When John visited the library he was informed he might obtain copies of these directories from the Post Office supplies department.

The Lord had already shown John that SOON was not to be a large organisation but instead was to provide an opportunity for Christians to serve Him in their spare time from home. After many years' experience as deputation secretary for WEC, John knew that enlisting volunteers was no easy matter! Humanly speaking, it seemed they were asking for the moon when they asked God to provide ten "SOON Service Corps" of groups or individuals who would be willing to wrap and post the broadsheet.

Volunteer typists would also be needed to prepare address labels to send to the groups. They would receive sections of the telephone directories obtained by John. These directories proved a valuable source for addresses of schools, colleges, hospitals and prisons. In addition, the Indian Post Office Guide publicised addresses of the 83,000 post offices in India. For many years, the Post Office Christian Association of Britain has helped in the distribution of broadsheets to their colleagues in India and other countries.

Across the United Kingdom, Christians caught the vision. Through their involvement they found fulfilment and God's purpose for them. Within a short time, the first ten SOON Service Corps were formed, and the dispatch machinery could go into operation. In those days each SOON Service Corps (now known as Despatch Units) received a map and the flag of the country to which they were sending the broadsheets. The groups met in homes, gathered around a table on which was a pile of *SOON!* broadsheets and a stack of address labels. As they folded, wrapped or pasted, they could also pray for those who would receive them.

Today there are over 1,000 Despatch Units. Every three months, families, church fellowships, youth and ladies' groups meet to prepare packages of *SOON!* for mailing. These are normally times of fellowship and fun as well as practical work!

When the printer's bill arrived, a few weeks after the despatch of that first edition, there was sufficient money in hand to meet the cost. Throughout that year, as each succeeding issue (of 15,000, 20,000 and then 30,000 copies) required more and more finance, John and Nellie were to experience the faithfulness of their miracle-working Director.

Chapter Two

A MAN PREPARED

John Lewis had been born in Upper Edmonton, North London. His parents were Anglicans and dedicated Sunday school teachers in the days when Sunday schools flourished. His mother supervised 300 children on Sunday mornings whilst another 500 attended 'Pa' Lewis's afternoon school. They had opportunity to influence many lives, not least that of young Gladys Aylward who was later to become world famous for her exploits in China.

As a young soldier during the First World War, Mr Lewis senior was already on a train bound for the Western Front and likely death when he was recalled. He was sent instead to Palestine where he stayed for a while after the war. Tales of his visits to Biblical sites in addition to various wartime escapades were recounted at every opportunity.

John's mother was greatly influenced by the teachings of Mrs Jessie Penn-Lewis, a forerunner of renewal insights. She regularly attended her meetings on the Thames Embankment. Later when the family moved to Leigh-on-Sea, Essex, they joined Christ Church, one of the few Free Churches of England. John responded to the gospel message at a meeting in a local cinema addressed by Lionel Fletcher, the Australian evangelist.

On leaving Westcliff High School, John took an accountancy post with a firm in London, entailing a sixty-mile round trip each day by train, and giving opportunity for his mind to devour the contents of many a book. The life story of C.T.Studd, the cricketer turned missionary, captivated his attention. "I never thought such a life was possible," John commented after reading his biography.

Always a keen hiker, John enjoyed many holidays on the Continent. An experience high in the Swiss Alps left an indelible imprint on his life. Suddenly faced with a dangerous situation, God challenged him concerning the risks he was taking. There and then he vowed to attend the Keswick meetings the following year, where its missionary-orientated programme presented the ideal opportunity for God to speak to him.

He received his first introduction to WEC when a friend took him along to the headquarters, where he met Norman Grubb, the British Director of WEC. John felt drawn towards missionary work, but first there had to be a time of preparation. Through reading a copy of the *Emmanuel Magazine* which came into his father's hands whilst he was considering his future, John was directed to study at the Emmanuel Bible College, where he came under the spiritual influence of the principal, J.D.Drysdale.

Medical work in India seemed to beckon, so a further period of training followed at the Missionary School of Medicine. Uncertain whether to continue and take a full medical course, John waited for the Lord to open up the way. WEC suggested he spend a year with the Friends Evangelistic Band in order to gain some experience in the field of evangelism. So, 1939 found him living in a caravan on a North Norfolk farm ministering to the three mission halls in the locality.

Exchanging his 'parish' for a desk, he then spent some time assisting with the administrative duties at WEC headquarters. Along with Norman Grubb and Fred Anthony, he would open the mail each day and together they sought the Lord's mind on any matters arising from it. Prayer was the focal point of their daily routine. "Everyone must attend prayers even if they get no dinner," ordered Mr Grubb. Those anointed prayer sessions had a profound effect on John. There he saw first hand just what God could do in response to the intercessions of His people. God was preparing His servant for the work with SOON.

During the war years, Ma and Pa Lewis were invited to join the team at WEC headquarters. Their job was to take charge of the catering and oversee the many day-to-day affairs of an ever-widening ministry. By then, Mr Lewis senior had retired from the Post Office and, as ever, was always ready for a challenge. So they gladly accepted this responsibility. He often recalled remarkable tales of faith experienced during those years with WEC, years when faith had been sorely tested, years when not one promise of the Heavenly Father ever failed.

Many were challenged by the lives and witness of this godly couple. Frequently, John's father could be seen pacing the streets of London's Soho and other parts of the metropolis. With a handful of gospel literature in many languages he seized every opportunity to share the good news of Jesus Christ. Mr Lewis's faith and love for the Lord, coupled with his enthusiasm to reach the lost, have been inherited by his son.

John had first met Nellie Harte at Emmanuel Bible College in 1936. They were married in 1942, and she took over as the Ladies' Candidate Secretary, a role for which her warm, endearing personality was ideally suited. Always hospitable, there was room in their hearts and home for all. John had moved into extension work in the home department of the WEC, a task that would keep him occupied for the next twenty years, until the new ministry of SOON called him.

John and Nellie Lewis in 1971

The long-awaited, easy-English broadsheet was making its way around the globe when disaster struck. Without warning, John Lewis suffered a heart attack, throwing the whole future of the new ministry into jeopardy. However, it was not John's work but God's work, and it had received His anointing. John was His instrument and as such was subject to divine authority. The One who allowed the blow to be struck was also the One to administer the balm. John was about to experience something of his Heavenly Father's care as never before.

"You must keep perfectly still; your life depends on it," the matron told John as he lay in the hospital in Upper Norwood. Each hour John prayed, "Lord, help me to remain still for this next hour." As he did so, the word of the

Lord came to him: "This sickness is not unto death but for the glory of God." John repeated those words to himself again and again.

God honoured His word. Two Christian friends, Peter Palmer and Jack Aitken, were asked to come and lay hands on John and anoint him with oil in the name of the Lord. As they prayed the prayer of faith, God touched John and the healing process began. The doctors were amazed. "We thought you had gone! You gave us such a shock." During the long road to recovery, John often reflected on the ministry to which God had so recently called him. Then the Lord gave him another promise: "I have set before you an open door and no man shall shut it." Here was confirmation that he would continue the ministry which God had given him.

"Strange that this should happen just as they were setting out to fulfil what God had revealed as His will for them," said some people when they heard what had happened. Others were of the opinion that the illness must have been the work of the enemy, who sought to thwart God's purposes in the ministry. As time went by the SOON team would experience many personal attacks from the evil one.

Whatever the reasons, God's methods are contrary to human thinking. Few expected the ministry to survive the crisis; but not only did it survive, it continued to thrive. In John's own words, "It was marvellous to see how God worked in spite of all that was levelled against this evangelistic broadsheet ministry at the beginning."

The SOON team in 1994. Left to right, back row: Peter Skinner, Tony Whittaker, Stan Leader, John Lewis, Geoff McEvansoneya, Peter Hopkins. Front row: Peggy Skinner, Mary Whittaker, Pauline Lewis, Angela McEvansoneya, Marie Hopkins.

Chapter Three

CHANGED LIVES

Early response indicated that *SOON!* was on target. "Without *SOON!* I would not have known the Lord," was typical of hundreds of letters received over the years. Copies have been known to exist long after distribution, which is some achievement for a sheet of paper. A coupon from a 1967 *SOON!* broadsheet was returned to the office in 1979. Issue 45 was still around nearly twenty years later, and an African from Sierra Leone wrote in October 1983 to say he had just received a copy of the May/June 1962 edition.

The life-saving message lives on even when the paper is discarded. "I would like a free *SOON!* and Bible course," wrote a Filipino student. "The coupon is stained because a single page of *SOON!* was used as a wrapper for the food I bought... I sat down on my bed and started reading the *SOON!* paper. It was just what I needed... *SOON!* will help me strengthen my faith towards the Holy God." One copy was discovered in a dustbin in Cameroon while another was picked up on a dusty road in Old Delhi. Each one made its mark. On one occasion, some broadsheets were stolen and as a result the thief found Christ!

An African student told how he went to the post office during his lunch break to collect his *SOON!*. Returning to school, he found the students rioting and the police singling out the troublemakers. Not wishing to be involved, he turned to run home. A policeman spotted him and threw him into the wagon without waiting for an explanation. While in his prison cell, he took out his copy of *SOON!* and read the testimonies to the other prisoners. Many listened and showed much interest as he witnessed for the Lord. After being held for a week, he had to appear in court. The other students paid fines before being released; but when the young Christian's name was called, he was told his fine had already been paid! He never knew who paid it.

Soon the need to extend to other countries became apparent. By the end of 1962, there were some twenty groups servicing twenty-three countries: Nyasaland, Kenya, Ghana, Vietnam, Uganda, Sierra Leone, Nigeria, West Indies, Gambia, Northern Rhodesia, Libya, Aden, Egypt, Liberia, Israel, Somalia, India, Ethiopia, Tanganyika, Ceylon, Thailand, Pakistan and Indonesia. Even in those early days the possibility of reaching the communist countries behind the Iron Curtain was considered. Issue by issue, the work expanded as inroads were made into new territory.

A letter from a Nigerian reader illustrates response from the Muslim world: "I am a Moslem but now I want to change to Christianity. Send me some books about Jesus Christ." Another wrote: "I am a Muslim, but I love the beautiful and heart-appealing teachings of Christianity in your paper." Others described *SOON!* as "the best magazine I have ever seen", or "the most interesting paper, one which can draw my attention towards God's call".

"Many will not listen to us. They just pass us by," wrote a Christian worker from Vietnam. "However, if we offer them an English leaflet, they grab it and eagerly read it."

Statistics indicate that no less than 1,000 million individuals use English as a first or second language and, with many educational establishments around the world now teaching English, the demand for suitable literature is insatiable. With its easy English, it is not surprising that the *SOON!* broadsheet became popular throughout the world.

Requests for the broadsheet flooded in. A distributor in Northern Rhodesia, thanking SOON for his consignment, said, "Of the 200 *SOON!* which I received this morning, 100 have already gone and I haven't even read it myself yet." This typified the dilemma of many recipients – there simply were not enough copies to go round. By the middle of 1964, 52,000 copies of each edition were printed and still rationing was necessary. Even today, with 750,000 copies printed per issue, a single broadsheet can often be read by as many as twenty people.

As the workload increased Eileen Fowler, who was in-

Distributing SOON! on a bus in Ghana

volved with the new broadsheet in Portuguese called *Cedo,* helped John and Nellie in the mornings. It became clear that more full-time workers were urgently needed in the office. So it was a great relief when, in direct answer to prayer, Colin and Winnie Tink joined the SOON team in September 1963.

Even with the additional staff, there was still a lot of work to be done, especially when the bimonthly consignments of *SOON!* arrived from the printers. John weighed out the broadsheets into 100s, 50s and 25s ready for distribution to the SOON Service Corps around the country. Colin wrapped and packed, while in another corner Winnie recorded all the relevant details. Every member of the team played their part to ensure that the 40,000 copies were despatched quickly and efficiently.

Students in East Africa who requested further information were referred to the Light of Life Bible Correspondence Course. For those living in West Africa, the Back to the Bible Broadcasting Association agreed to send their courses. In addition, a short leaflet in simple English entitled *A Changed Life For You* was sent to all who responded.

By the close of 1963 an average of five responses per day were reaching SOON. "Try to help me by all means. I want to become a Christian," wrote a man from Sierra Leone. "How can I become a new man? I am at present a lover of alcohol. I want to stop this. How can I?" was the plea of Rusadene, a Nigerian. Another reader in Accra wrote, "Please enrol me as one of your students, because I want a change of life." Such encouragement was welcome.

The first two years had certainly not been easy. For one thing, the tiny office at the rear of WEC's main building was far from ideal for the growing ministry. A recurring topic at the SOON prayer meetings was the need for improved office accommodation. Consideration was given to various properties, in particular Vicotts, a country house in Bolney, Sussex owned by Mr Harry Henley, a market gardener. However, the way ahead remained unclear.

Vicotts, SOON headquarters, 1964

Twelve months elapsed before an unexpected early morning phone call was received renewing the offer. The timing was perfect, for the team had arranged to view some property in Brighton later that day. A simple diversion en route enabled them to visit Vicotts. Mr Henley was anxious for the premises to be used for the Lord's work. This time God said, "Yes!"

Removal plans were set in motion immediately. April 1964 found a small band of faithful workers heading for a new home in the tranquil surroundings of the Sussex countryside. What a contrast to the hubbub of the capital and the cramped conditions of their former office! Much needed to be done, as the house had been uninhabited for three years.

An enthusiastic group from WEC headquarters spent that Easter decorating and making the necessary alterations. One of them, Bill Aitken, gallantly volunteered to decorate the staircase. Suddenly, the plank on which he was standing snapped and Bill's six-foot form landed in a crumpled heap on the floor. He spent the next few months with his leg in plaster. The accident did nothing to deter him from later joining the team full time!

To accommodate the whole team and provide office space, the house required some modifications. Upstairs rooms were partitioned, thereby making two rooms into four. This task was undertaken by Derek Smith, a trained carpenter from WEC, assisted by his brother Paul and Colin Tink.

The extensive grounds at Vicotts made it possible for the team to grow their own vegetables. A brood of chickens ensured a daily supply of fresh eggs and any surplus was sold to the locals to help offset the cost of the chicken food. Coming from a country background, Colin soon found himself responsible for looking after the poultry and the garden. Trundling barrow loads of cow manure from a nearby farm provided him with welcome breaks from office routine!

Letters and coupons arrived daily from all parts of the world. A letter from Vietnam requested, "Please send *SOON!* for our Reading Rooms in Saigon, Hue and Da Nang." Another, from Thailand, spoke of the hunger to know more. Many showed genuine concern for their spiritual state. "I would like my life to be changed. I have been committing sins and would like them to go away."

Then there was the testimony of an ex-drug addict and

prisoner who, having lost his wife, was too depressed to go home to his own country. One day he saw a five-year-old girl reading a copy of *SOON!* and asked if he could have it. She gave it to him and it changed his life. In India, a man was walking along a mountain path intending to commit suicide when a torn piece of paper with a red flash caught his attention. His life was saved by this fragment of *SOON!* which gave him fresh hope.

The Lord added more personnel to the team. Mary Pritchard was led into the work during her last year at Bible school in 1964. God spoke to her very clearly through 'the writer's inkhorn' in Ezekiel 9:3, and confirmed it through a friend who knew nothing about her thoughts. She stayed with SOON for twelve years before moving on to work with the immigrant community in Britain. As she saw the work grow year by year, she began to realise how big God is, and also how big the world is!

As the work expanded, even more space was needed. Mr Henley offered the use of an outbuilding alongside his farm shop just down the road. So, together with their typewriters and two huge rotary card indexes, Winnie and Mary moved into their new office. Two oil heaters were installed to give relief from the freezing temperature in winter. Returning one day after lunch, Winnie and Mary opened the door to find the room full of dense smoke. The ceiling was festooned with two-foot-long black cobwebs and everything, including the card index, was blackened. Only the Lord prevented what could have been a catastrophe.

By the end of that year, 60,000 copies of *SOON!* were being distributed bimonthly, with Greenland and Iceland added to the countries already supplied. With many more SOON Service Corps in operation, Colin Tink travelled widely in his little grey Austin to encourage them and interest others in the work. When Bill Aitken joined the team, he undertook much of the deputation and aimed to visit all sending groups at least once a year. The blessings of fellowship with other believers on those trips alleviated the tedious journeys in the days when almost the only motorway was the M1.

In May 1973 Ron and Connie Currey joined the SOON team, taking early retirement from local government in order to do so. Ron brought to the SOON ministry a mind for effective operating structures, and set up the framework for the SOON Despatch Unit ministry which continues to this day. Connie wrote a script for the SOON audio-visual slide set, which is still in use. Ron retired from the work in 1981.

Chapter Four

A MULTI-NATIONAL BIBLE SCHOOL

As the number of broadsheets increased, so the responses also became more numerous. For some time, the need for an easy-English Bible course had been apparent. But who was the man for the job? David Wallington had worked with the United Bible Societies as assistant editor of *The Bible Translator*. During that time he developed an interest in easy English.

One day, while reading 1 Corinthians 14 on his way to work, the phrase 'words easy to be understood' stood out. It prompted him to write an article on the need for simplified versions of Scripture. When the article was printed in 1961, David sent copies to all the missionary organisations and Bible schools in England thinking they would all recognise the importance of the subject. He expected a flood of response, but only one person showed any interest - John Lewis of WEC! They arranged to meet and as a result it was suggested that David prepare a Bible course in simplified English.

The course had to be tailored to meet the situation. When John had looked at the Bible courses already available, he found they were purely doctrinal, assuming the student already had a knowledge of the Bible. Such courses would be unsuitable for those whose holy book might be the Qu'ran. Because few readers of *SOON!* had access to a Bible, the relevant Scriptures would have to be quoted in the study books.

Muslims, Hindus, Buddhists and even atheists received copies of *SOON!*. Designing a course which was relevant to all their different needs was no easy matter. However, after prayerful consideration, David thought of Psalm 1, which shows that happiness comes from obeying God. So the topic for the first lesson was, 'You can be happy.' The second lesson, raising the question of sin, asked, 'Are you happy?' and the third, entitled 'Jesus can make you happy', dealt with the truth about Jesus. The Bible passages were simplified and any difficult words explained.

The second part of the ten-lesson course was based on Mark's Gospel. Here, incidents which demonstrate the Lord's ability to heal and release people from the bondage of evil spirits were particularly appropriate to those influenced by tribal culture and ancestral worship.

Eventually the draft of the first course arrived on John's desk. Again, God's timing proved to be perfect. The arrival of the draft coincided with an apologetic letter from the Back to the Bible Broadcasting Association. It said, "Sorry! We have been flooded with requests for Bible courses. We simply can't cope!" Soon an old Gestetner was churning out the first copies of *Teach Yourself the Good Life*.

The price of that first course was three shillings, but now all courses are free of charge because many students have no means of paying. Some will even go without a meal to find the price of a stamp. Students who successfully completed a Bible course were awarded certificates, which are highly valued in developing nations.

The excitement of witnessing more and more courses

being mailed day after day was tempered by the realisation that what goes out, must come back! By this time, the Bible Course office had been relocated to another property in Bolney which had been made available by the owner, Miss Haslett. A spare bedroom became the hub of the rapidly-expanding follow-up work.

In the first year, 1,000 students registered from dozens of countries. A multi-national Bible school had been founded. Some wrote with difficult questions. The son of a witch doctor became a Christian. He asked, "The Bible says I should obey my father, but what should I do when my father tells me to collect herbs for his witchcraft?"

Bible course student, Nigeria

Questions concerning the Trinity, creation and the Sabbath were frequently asked.

Many, concerned about salvation, ask, "How can I know I'm saved?" A Kenyan lady wrote, "I am really lost! Help me! Show me the way to follow." As the students discover the truth of God's Word, many are challenged about their relationship with Jesus Christ. A Hindu Brahmin wrote, "This course has helped me come to know a lot about Christianity. I'll try my best to follow these teachings." Another student, Albert Ombrogo, returning his course for marking, commented, "I never believed that Jesus can heal and help when one has problems, but now I believe and I know that Jesus helps and he has got a plan for everybody."

In 1965, Margaret Brown, a former missionary in Pakistan and Kashmir, returned to Britain and started helping in the office two days a week. While working with the Pakistan Bible Correspondence School in Abbottabad she had found it useful to have literature in English. This she could send to students who were struggling to gain an elementary knowledge of the language. *SOON!* had been a natural choice. Her help came at the right time because amazing acceleration occurred in that year, resulting in the dispatch of 10,000 Bible courses.

Over the next few years, additional courses were produced. Course Two deals with sinful things which can cause unhappiness. Growth in the Christian life is the main topic considered in Course Three. Later, a study of the letter of James was added. A few modifications have been necessary, but basically the courses remain much the same and continue to provide teaching which can be readily understood.

As may be expected, some students do not proceed beyond the first course. Although some lose interest, others simply may not have enough money to pay the return postage. For those in India, a postbox address within the country reduces the cost to the student. Similar arrangements are now made for other countries where foreign postage has become too expensive, such as Nigeria and the former USSR.

From the outset, the courses were warmly received. A student in Mauritius said, "Since taking your course, I have repented of my sins. I have turned away from them and lead a good life." A prisoner in Uganda thanked SOON for his Bible course. He said, "I have been a sinner, but now realise what God is able to do for me."

Nurse Mary Adebola has completed all four
SOON Bible courses

Initially, Colin Tink had the unenviable task of marking the Bible courses in between his commitments on the deputation side. He recalls returning from a ten-day visit to Northern Ireland to be confronted with an enormous pile of envelopes, beneath which was a desk – somewhere! Evidently something had to be done. In keeping with John's vision that the Lord's people could be involved in their spare time, it seemed the time had come to delegate the responsibility for marking the courses. However, employing Christians of varying denominations could create problems. Some, with their own particular theological bias, might attempt to propagate their own theories and cause confusion. After much prayer, John and his team felt they could trust the Lord to take care of any problems which might arise.

Spare-time Bible Course markers send the courses on a monthly basis to the students allocated to them. A late-evening visitor to the home of one of these markers would not imagine that the cosy living room was part of a multinational Bible school. While another man might relax in front of the television after a tiring shift at the local factory, this man takes a box file, labelled 'SOON Courses', from the cupboard. Then, instead of settling himself in an easy chair, he sits at the table and looks at the courses that have been sent for marking.

The first one is from a student in northern Nigeria. Moses has completed the first two Bible courses and shown much interest. For the first time, he has read about Jesus coming back again. There are few mistakes, so he has obviously understood the lesson. But he is still puzzled. "If Jesus is coming back for the Christians, who will come for the Moslems?" Before doing anything else, the marker bows his head in prayer. He does not wish to offend. Carefully choosing his words, he writes a few short sentences in reply and then looks for a suitable booklet from the collection in his file. A small leaflet entitled *The Second Coming of Christ* catches his eye. He places the tract with the course, completes a certificate and enters the student's mark on his record card. The lesson, along with a copy of the next one, is now ready for mailing.

The marker turns his attention to the next paper on the pile, from a young lady in Hungary who is doing Course One. She explains that she loves the English language but finds it hard to understand why anyone should want to believe in Jesus Christ. Despite the accuracy of her answers, it is obvious that she is still confused by ideologies and man-made religions. The marker intercedes for her, too, asking God to show her that her real need is Jesus.

The next two papers are quite straightforward with the exception of a few indecipherable words. The marker yawns and glances at the clock – it is time for bed. The other courses can wait until tomorrow. He will drop the completed courses in the letter box on his way to work in the morning. Just before turning out the light he reads a short passage from Isaiah: 'Blessed are you who sow beside all waters.' As he drifts off to sleep, he thinks, "I suppose that's just what I'm doing, and what joy it gives me!"

Many have found fulfilment in the work of SOON. Christians unable to serve overseas have been thrilled to have the opportunity to make contact with those in distant countries. Despite being at home, they have been able to reach those in spiritual darkness with the gospel message. The words of Jesus in the Sermon on the Mount, "Give and it will be given to you..." has added a new dimension to many as they have given themselves in the service of others. It also has tremendous therapeutic value. The lonely and depressed find friendship by linking up with others to form a Despatch Unit. The unemployed are redeployed in God's service and thus fill the void which once existed. Retirees and young mums caring for families have all found satisfaction in this exciting ministry. As one helper remarked, "My greatest joy is to point someone to the Saviour." It has been said that "the only ability God requires is availability", a fact proved true by the countless SOON helpers.

No threat of redundancy overshadows this work. Retirement years have been so transformed that many elderly folk are too busy to die! One man was still marking courses when he went to be with the Lord in his ninetieth year.

Does the ministry of SOON end with the conversion of students? By no means. "*SOON!* is a candle flame in this dark world," wrote a young man. When such a flame is ignited by God it can never be extinguished.

Chapter Five

TEAM WORK

For ten years, the offices at Vicotts throbbed with a thriving ministry. Then the unexpected death of Mr Henley in 1973 meant that the premises had to be vacated. The SOON team felt this was the time to trust the Lord for a larger building. Urgent prayer was requested. At the WEC Kilcreggan holiday centre, a couple from Willington in Derbyshire heard of their need. Oliver and Joyce Eley owned 'Vere Lodge', a spacious, early Victorian house with a separate stable block converted into living accommodation.

They no longer needed such a large house and were considering making it available for the Lord's work. After the Lord spoke to them individually, they agreed to offer the property to SOON at the same price for which they had purchased it in 1966, well below the current market value. The financial resources of SOON were little more than they had been in 1963. Yet again, the Lord worked. In answer to prayer He provided the finance to purchase the house.

Vere Lodge was ideal. Even the name 'House of Verity' suggested that it had been built for Christians. Three stained-glass panes set in a large window on the stairs supported this idea. They portrayed the *Mayflower*, the Edinburgh home of John Knox, and William Caxton. It seems appropriate that the truth of God's Word should still shine from the house.

On a cold November day in 1974 a procession of vehicles made its way up the motorway to the Midlands. A work team also travelled up from Sussex to help with the necessary alterations. Oliver Eley helped to build a kitchenette in one of the upstairs rooms, making a bedsitter for Mary Pritchard. In the grounds they erected the ex-mission hall which had been transported from Bolney where it had been used as the main office. For a time, the Eleys remained in 'Vere Cottage', the converted stable-block.

SOON had been in Willington for twelve months when the team was augmented by Tony and Mary Whittaker. This couple had formed a Despatch Unit, sending copies of *SOON!* to one hundred addresses in Ghana. Now they believed the Lord wanted them to be involved full time in the work. For a few weeks Tony commuted to and fro as he helped prepare their accommodation in Vere Lodge.

When the rooms were ready the new workers moved in with their two children, Wendy and Brian.

Later, the Whittakers did a course at Birmingham Bible Institute followed by a few months at WEC headquarters for assessment and training before becoming permanent members of the team.

Unloading bulk supplies of SOON!

A year after Tony joined the team, he received a letter from a *SOON!* reader asking for information about a certain Christian magazine. The query led to a chain of events that the reader could not have imagined. Tony did not have the information, but remembered that a student he had known at Bristol University had once mentioned the magazine. He wrote to him care of the university, hoping it would eventually reach him. At the same time he enclosed some literature about SOON.

Tony's letter arrived when Geoff McEvansoneya was praying about serving the Lord in his spare time. Lecturing at a London college not only gave him long holidays, but also involved an hour's train journey twice a day. As he read the information about SOON he saw this could be the answer to his prayers. In addition to starting a Despatch Unit, Geoff undertook typing and marking. Before long he felt God wanted him to become involved on a full-time basis. His wife Angela, however, had doubts, believing her ministry should be among elderly people and young children. She also had a special burden for the millions of people in China. In addition they were both happily settled in their local church in Haslemere, Surrey, and had three small children.

Two months later, Geoff attended a SOON reunion at Bolney where Nellie Lewis challenged the younger men to help in the work. This confirmed to Geoff what he already knew – that God wanted him in SOON. Back at home Angela, too, received a clear word from the Lord that their future lay with SOON. So, under totally different circumstances, the Holy Spirit united their two hearts with one desire – to serve God in the SOON ministry.

John Lewis' daughter, Pauline, has been closely associated with SOON from the beginning. Even when she was nursing she often spent her days off helping out in the office. Having completed her Midwifery course, she felt led to offer to help on a full-time basis for a while. By 1974, she was convinced that God wanted her to continue in Christian work rather than return to nursing. So a period at Redcliffe Bible College followed. During this time, the Lord confirmed that her future lay with SOON. Isaiah 55:10-11 made a particular impression on her. Here the Lord promises to prosper His word wherever it goes – a promise that Pauline was to see fulfilled time and again in the ministry of SOON.

However, at the end of her Bible training, Pauline found her nursing skills required at home. First she took care of her grandfather until he went to be with the Lord in 1977.

Then it was her mother who needed care. This went on until May 1981 when Nellie was called Home.

Today, Pauline is in charge of the Bible courses. With 300 Bible Course markers to supervise, she has little time for relaxation. In addition she also has many 'behind the scenes' jobs such as providing hospitality to the many visitors to Vere Lodge.

One day in April the team were enjoying their morning coffee break when Pauline received an official-looking letter from the council. The letter explained that, due to over-loading of the drains, it was necessary to institute a wash-ing rota in Willington. Under certain bye-laws it would only be possible to use the washing machine once a week at a specified time. The time allocated to Pauline was between 10 and 12 on Sunday morning.

Normally a placid person, Pauline was indignant at be-ing allocated a time when she expected to be at church. The team shared her indignation and encouraged her to ring the office to arrange a swap. The official on the other end of the line agreed to make the necessary arrange-ments. At that point muffled laughter, and the rapid exit of certain members of staff, made Pauline realise she had been expertly April-fooled!

April Fools' Day is not the only time when it is helpful to see the funny side of a situation. Tony recalls an occa-sion when he climbed a ladder to remove debris from the guttering. Suddenly he was showered with leaves and muddy water from which there was no escape.

Working closely together as a team requires a great deal of patience and understanding. Each working day starts with a staff prayer meeting in the lounge. These meetings help to set the tone of the day. No problem is too great or too mundane for the ear of God. It is not always easy to ensure that all parts of the vast machinery operate smoothly. Knowing that the Lord's will is paramount, some-times it is necessary to delay a decision until a consensus of opinion can be reached under the guiding hand of the Holy Spirit. At ten o'clock the staff disperse to their offices.

In his office on the ground floor, John attends to the layout of the forthcoming broadsheet. An assortment of testimonies from a variety of journals lie on the desk await-ing his consideration. The typewriter is rarely silent. Dur-ing his lunch break he exchanges his desk for the garden. Lawns have to be cut, borders weeded and the vegetable plot tended. John has found this brief hour to be physi-cally beneficial as well as giving him an additional inter-est and diversion.

In his first-floor office, Geoff sorts the incoming mail ready to pass it on to the appropriate departments. With around 2,000 letters arriving each week, opening the mail can be a lengthy procedure. The task is shared by Stan Leader, who formerly worked in Thailand as a WEC mis-sionary, and by Peter Skinner, a music teacher who joined the team in 1993. Bulky packages are treated with cau-tion. One contained a furry tail obviously intended as a talisman. It was not kept!

Amazingly, letters bearing no more than the words 'SOON, England' find their way to their intended destina-tion. More bizarre examples have included 'Mr Willing' or even 'The Queen of England, London'.

Letters request not only broadsheets, but also Bible courses, pen friends and audio-cassettes of *SOON!* Some carry reports of the blessing readers have received through the broadsheet. Others may require a personal reply. Mary Whittaker processes these and passes them on to one of her team of 'problem-letter writers'. Certain requests are impossible to satisfy. One time a text quoted on the broadsheets referred to the blood of Christ. As a result, some students wrote in asking to be sent a bottle of Jesus' blood.

The team is augmented by part-time volunteers whose jobs include packing parcels and sorting out the cassette requests. One regular helper until 1994 was Vic Genders. Then the Lord chose to call him Home suddenly while he was working at Vere Lodge. He had been greatly used to develop the audio-cassette aspect of the ministry.

Team work underlies every aspect of SOON. It is impossible to mention everyone who has been prompted by God to play a role in this ministry over the past thirty years. Other missions have also contributed much to the broadsheet ministry.

Members of the Christian Publicity Organisation, based at Worthing, view the printing of gospel broadsheets as a major part of their contribution to world mission. Through 'Project Print' they seek to alleviate the hunger for literature which exists in many areas of the world. CPO was established in 1956 by Alan Baird, John Milne and David Armstrong. By 1965 the WEC Press was unable to keep up the pace of printing the broadsheets so CPO offered to help. This forged a partnership which continues to this day. Knowing that Fred Chapman was trusting the Lord to meet the financial needs of the Bientôt ministry, they offered to print 10,000 copies of *Bientôt* on a 'cost of materials plus ten per cent only' basis. This is still the policy for all the gospel broadsheets printed there.

In 1968, CPO agreed to assist with the bimonthly printing of up to 100,000 copies per issue of both *SOON!* and *Bientôt.* By 1973, they were printing 400,000 copies per quarter. Ten years later the figure had risen to over 500,000 *SOON!* broadsheets per issue. Now, four million gospel broadsheets, including *Bientôt* and *Upesi* (Swahili), are printed each year, making the broadsheet ministry an integral part of CPO.

As the quantities increased, so CPO's faith was stretched. They have experienced God's faithfulness in many wonderful ways, enabling them to continue on the same basis for over twenty-five years. As labour costs continually rise, this sacrificial act on the part of the CPO team has undoubtedly been a major part of God's provision for SOON. With the Bible Course ministry also growing at a remarkable rate, CPO has found it necessary to reprint the first part of the Course many times.

Another mission working closely with SOON is the Gospel Printing Mission founded by David Cotton. While attending a WEC meeting, David was challenged when he heard how communists used literature to promote their cause. He began to recognise the need for short, easy-English gospel leaflets for overseas use. Further visits to WEC headquarters endorsed the vision God had given him. His workshop was the garden shed and he used a primitive hand machine to print the simple leaflets. Encouragement from John Lewis and others at WEC headquarters helped overcome the many discouragements he faced in the early months.

Not surprisingly, he developed links with the SOON ministry. The Gospel Printing Mission prepared such leaflets as *The Christian and his Saviour, The Christian and his Bible* and *The Christian and his Church*. They also printed the *Your Questions Answered* series which has proved so useful to Bible Course markers and Readers Club Advisors. *SOON!* articles which have shown a good response have also been reproduced by GPM in the form of tracts.

All GPM literature is distributed free of charge. Like

SOON, the mission does not make any appeals for funds. They look to God alone to supply the ever-increasing costs.

Operation Mobilisation have often reprinted copies of *SOON!* for use on their ships. Team members distribute them at their ports of call along with other literature. Following a visit by *Logos II* in 1990, the response from the USSR increased by about 600 per cent. One of those contacted was Lasmane. "Today I was at the ship *Logos II* and I got this free copy of *SOON!* God has changed my life by giving me the power of His Spirit," he wrote.

Operation Mobilisation also co-operated with SOON in 1965 to print *Good News for the World*, a simplified New Testament in worldwide English prepared by Miss Annie Cressman who had been a missionary in Liberia. This version was largely used in the SOON Bible courses, and there are plans for a new edition to be published by the Evangel Publishing House of Nairobi, Kenya.

Another key task is carried out by Jack Simpson of Poole, who despatches New Testaments to Club Leaders and Bible Course markers. A small, cheap edition of the *New International Version* has been extensively used for this purpose, but it is hoped that the Cressman version in simpler English will be widely used when it becomes available again.

At international events, such as the Olympic Games, Christian workers from various organisations such as Youth With A Mission have used special editions of *SOON!* as part of their evangelistic outreach to people from many nations.

Because expansion on the outreach side of the ministry needs to be matched by increased prayer and practical help by Christians in the United Kingdom and elsewhere, deputation is a vital aspect of the work. Up-to-date reports allow churches and fellowships across the country to share in the joy of what God is doing around the world.

John and his daughter Pauline are responsible for many of these meetings. They welcome opportunities to promote the work at Christian conferences, church services, university and college Christian Unions. Visual displays and missionary stands all help to demonstrate the impact of the ministry. Now with a twenty-minute video presentation *In Simple Words* and a set of acetates for the overhead projector, the SOON ministry can be shared with a wider audience.

John's infectious enthusiasm and passionate concern for the extension of God's kingdom is hard to ignore. Those listening to him are stirred and challenged by the reports of people turning to Christ, especially when it happens in countries normally closed to missionaries. Across Britain, and even in some countries of Europe, people of all ages have caught the vision of what God can do through the printed page to transform lives and bring healing and happiness to many. When this vision is combined with the Holy Spirit's gentle prompting, Christians are driven to pray, to give, or to become involved in a practical way.

CPO - printers of SOON!

Chapter Six

MOVING AHEAD

Every SOON Bible Course student is encouraged to share the good news of Jesus Christ with their friends and family. Forming a SOON Readers Club is one way of doing that. Regular club meetings give an opportunity to read and discuss the articles in *SOON!*, and enable members to study the Bible courses with the aid of notes. Every Bible Course student who successfully completes all four SOON Bible courses, and gives testimony to a changed life through Jesus Christ, is viewed as a potential club leader.

It was on a visit by John and Nellie Lewis to Uganda that the club vision really came alive. In almost every village they found clubs – 'Top Life Club' or a 'New Life Club'. It seemed all Africans wanted to belong to clubs. Even before the club ministry was officially launched, letters were arriving at headquarters saying, "I have started a SOON Readers Club in my village." By 1965, with one or two requests a day reaching the office, SOON Readers Clubs were officially established as part of the ongoing ministry. The following letter from Kenya was typical: "*SOON!* has helped me very much. Now I am changed. I can speak to God. I was a bad person who liked drink and dances. Now I am telling people the word of God. I want to start a SOON Readers Club."

In a very short time, groups had sprung up all over the world. Now there is at least one club in over twenty countries, including Albania, Bulgaria, China, the Czech Republic, Ethiopia, Iran, Kuwait, Latvia, Pakistan, Poland, Sudan, Turkey and Zaire. The two leading countries are Nigeria with over 500 clubs and Zimbabwe with 200.

Not all call themselves a SOON Readers Club. Among the more unusual titles are, The Royal Family, *Flamme de Feu* (Flame of Fire), Cry for India, and Christ's Ambassadors. They recognise that as representatives of the King of Kings, energised by the power of the Holy Spirit, they have a part to play in the extension of God's Kingdom.

John Attah was holding one of his many weekly club meetings. Although it was sundown, it was still very hot in the tin-roofed, mud church in Ashanti, Ghana. But all the members of his SOON Readers Club were there. He knew they would come. They always came when he rang the big bell each evening to announce the start of the Club meeting. Now he was waiting for the answers to his questions. "How can you be a strong Christian?" "What are the most important things in life?"

That day, as often, he had finished his work early in order to visit his Club members in their homes. Since he had become a Club Leader, his reputation in the village had been greatly enhanced. The ability to read simple English fluently opened doors to every home and heart. On his visits, he often started the conversation with "And what are your particular problems just now?" He knew that a ready, sympathetic ear was always acceptable to the Ghanaian villager. "Shall we pray together about the problem?" he would ask gently. "And listen, you are not the only one. Here are people with problems, too." Then he would read to them from his copy of *SOON!*. The testimonies were what they wanted to hear most: stories of deliverance from fear, sin and superstition.

Evenings spent together around the oil lamp were the highlight of the day. Whole families came along to read *SOON!* together and discuss the Bible study courses. "But how was Jesus a greater teacher than anyone else?" someone asked. "Why didn't Jesus make his teaching easier to understand?" John looked at the man who had asked the questions, wondering if he understood the true message yet: Jesus, Teacher, Saviour, King. At nightfall the group broke up and wandered off to their homes. As John watched them disappear into the darkness he wondered how long it would be before some of them would be able to lead a club of their own.

John Attah, overseer of clubs in Ghana

Formerly a cocoa farmer, John Attah has developed a full-time ministry to SOON clubs in Ghana. Trusting in God for his support, and with the aid of a motorbike provided by Christians in the UK, he visits clubs to check their progress. He may discover that there have been serious problems which the local leader cannot handle. With his God-given abilities, he seeks to help and advise. He never leaves without sharing the message of God's love and forgiveness. A man with a tremendous burden for his people, John's desire is to see at least ten souls won for the Lord every day!

In his own words he describes this ambition. "I know God's way is the best way. I want to be a man of prayer, a soul-winner and a blessing. I want to be a humble servant of God and do His will. Where He leads me, I will follow. It is our responsibility as Christians to carry this glorious gospel to the ends of the earth, where His name is not known. God's Word says, 'Where there is no vision, people perish.' That is the reason I have given myself completely to the Lord, for His work, that I might have some souls 'plucked from the burning' to lay at my Saviour's feet. This is the greatest business in the world - to lead men and women from darkness into His glorious light."

Reports of John's work in Ghana are often thrilling, as shown by the following account.

"At Anyinam: We travelled through deep forest into the interior. Finally we arrived at the destination and tears flowed freely as the converts surrounded us. Two policemen with loaded rifles and fixed bayonets were present to watch and listen at every meeting. Long tables were placed in the open air, from which we were served with thick slices of black bread and raw herring, boiled eggs and wild honey. A countless number of flies swarmed over everything. That night the women slept in the barn, and the men side by side like sardines, about 100 of us. Sunday morning a mighty revival swept the audience, so that hundreds fell on their faces and wept before the Lord.

"At Konongo: Next morning we held our service in one of the churches, where I spoke on the Holy Spirit. At the close, a woman came quickly to the front to ask forgiveness of two whom she had wronged. Scores knelt at the altar weeping and praying, utterly unconscious of those around. Sins were confessed and many bitter tears shed. My heart was deeply stirred as I listened to the plaintive tones of both men and women seeking God. The Spirit of God moved upon all hearts that morning, and for almost four hours the service continued with intense fervour.

"At all these places we had lack of copies of *SOON!* to give to others…"

Another time John Attah described how he handed out copies during a long train journey. "I spent about ten hours on the night train as the train did not go faster. When the train pulled out of the station in Kumasi, this was the signal for me to begin my distribution throughout the eight coaches. There were babies crying and being fed, people were chatting or calling each other, women were lodging their baskets overflowing with produce on the overcrowded luggage rack above my head, and young men were squeezing past in an effort to sell their cold drinks. Despite all this noise and bustle, some people were already settling down to sleep. I distributed two boxes of *SOON!*. The next day I took the Takoradi night train to Accra and did the same. Many accepted Christ Jesus as their personal Saviour and promised to write for a SOON Bible course."

Not all his reports are as dramatic as these, but the Lord is certainly using him greatly in connection with the SOON clubs.

More John Attahs are needed for this ministry – men and women with a compassion for souls who will visit and encourage the clubs. National believers have the advantage that they understand the culture, so misunderstandings are less likely.

Other letters reporting spiritual and numerical growth are also a source of much rejoicing. Opportunities to witness are eagerly pursued, as shown by this letter from Ellioth in Malawi: "We usually meet at our clubhouse and sometimes arrange journeys into the villages. We spend some days there, preaching and singing gospel songs and during weekends we go to preach in the markets, hospitals and community centres." Music plays an important part in African culture, so clubs in many of the townships and villages have their own choirs.

A report from Emmanuel Bannie shows the wide variety of members in clubs. "There are about forty members. They go to rural areas to preach and distribute tracts. Now the chief and the queen in the town are members of the club, and even they joined their activities. When consulted, they said, 'There is no king or queen in God's work. Everyone is working for his or her own crown from the Lord.'"

Many club leaders still attend school, so meetings have to be scheduled to fit in with their school timetable. Some clubs have three or four members, but others report that they have hundreds! At first the SOON team wondered whether some of these reports were exaggerated, but the way opened up for first Mary Pritchard, and later Pauline Lewis, to visit some of the clubs in West Africa. They found it was true that some clubs had hundreds of members and were virtually churches. For example, Anthony King of Côte d'Ivoire started with a Club, then formed a Sunday school, a day school and a church!

Finding a suitable venue for so many people may prove difficult. Club meetings in Africa are often held in the shade of palm branches. A few clubs use local church buildings. The first club that Pauline visited in Ghana met on a roof top! David Bensah's Club in Ghana have built their own meeting place.

Anthony King with his school

Readers Clubs are also formed in prisons. Kingsley Monde was converted while in a condemned cell at Kabwe Prison, Zambia. He completed the SOON Bible Course and then started a SOON Readers Club in his section of the prison. Out of ten other condemned prisoners only one failed to accept the Lord before being executed. Kingsley was also executed, but he died rejoicing in the Lord and wearing his usual big smile right to the end.

Visiting Kenya in 1988 gave John and Pauline Lewis the chance to meet thirty club leaders. The uncomfortable experience of travelling by *matatu*, a kind of converted pick-up truck, was tempered with the joy of Christian fellowship and the taste of African hospitality. In

Kakamega, they heard of twenty-seven clubs in that area alone.

Recently, the Kenyan Government has insisted that all clubs must be registered. This has often created problems and as a result some clubs have disbanded. However, issuing club certificates has helped to alleviate the problem.

If club leaders are to be effective evangelists they need sound teaching. Few have access to any Bible teaching aids. The SOON team ensure that every leader has a New Testament. In addition, Bible study notes and a copy of *LOOK* are sent to all those who register. *LOOK* is an easy-English broadsheet designed to bring an awareness of world mission to Christians in Third World countries. Daily Bible reading notes are also welcomed.

In 1966 it was decided that the best way to help and encourage club leaders was by giving each of them a club advisor to whom they could write when they had problems. The advisors befriend the leaders allocated to them and seek to maintain regular contact. Some leaders face much opposition and value the support of club advisors. From Northern Nigeria one leader wrote telling of the traumatic situation they were facing: "I regret to tell you that a number of my club members have been killed, and that the parents of other members have been killed, and many of my members are in dire straits."

Some club members display tremendous boldness in their efforts to share the gospel. Here is a letter from a club leader called Andrew, from Nigeria: "There was one juju man inside our village. This man he don't want to hear a man that is called Jesus. When you go to his compound, he may harass you or he will poison you. So one day, I took a Bible with me and my three members we went to his compound. This man cry out and call his gods that they should harm us but as soon as I call Jesus name, the man was silent. We came to him and I ask him, 'Who made you?' and 'Do you know the man called Jesus?' This man was confused, so I pray for him and told him to destroy all his gods and come to church. The man was later baptised and is in our midst."

Jesus cautioned His disciples, "Be wise as serpents and harmless as doves." This is good advice for any would-be club advisor. Tackling difficult questions posed by club leaders calls for tact and diplomacy. "I want to marry a girl from another tribe, but my parents won't allow it – what should I do?" asked a young African. Sometimes club members ask questions that their leader is unable to answer because his Bible knowledge is limited. If no one else can help him he will turn to his advisor for counselling.

Being a club advisor has its lighter moments. Somewhere in Africa is a child called Phillip A.G. Kelly, named after the advisor who corresponded with his father. Another advisor received a marriage proposal!

Today the responsibility for the Clubs has been taken over by Peter Hopkins, a former TV transmission engineer and manager, who joined the SOON team in 1992. He is entering all the clubs onto a computer database. Already he has listed over 8,000 clubs which have existed over the years. Of course, some may have ceased functioning since they started, but nearly 2,000 are known to have been recently active, and more are constantly coming to light.

As the clubs grew, some have become established churches. A paper entitled *The True Christian Church* was prepared for the guidance of their leaders. It provides basic teaching about the nature of the local church, and urges leaders to seek fellowship with other Bible-based churches. It also enables club leaders to instruct members who have been exposed to false teaching from the cults. *Teach Yourself* papers on specific topics – Prayer, the Bible and the Holy Spirit – were produced with the help of Doug Harris, connected with Halford House, Richmond.

In Malawi, about thirty miles from Blantyre, is a church with 5,000 members, led by Pastor Nazombe. They received virtually all their teaching from *SOON!* and *LOOK.*

In 1993 came news of a church which reputedly has 28,000 members. This is an extract from a report by ex-SOON Bible Course markers, Arnold and June Hall, now living in Zimbabwe.

"The church is in Buhera, 300 miles from Bulawayo, and 40 miles from the nearest tarred road. The people in this region are subsistence farmers – their main preoccupation is to stay alive. Thousands of them died in last year's drought.

"The church was started in September 1992. The leader is twenty-three-year-old Situta, a SOON Bible Course student, assisted by his brother aged 20. The church has 23 centres in a 15-mile radius. Masasa village was one such meeting place. They had had 1,600 people gathered waiting for us from 7am to 5pm in the market place. During that time 500 people had preached to the crowd.... Several local thieves have heard the Word and repented. This has made the group popular with the local headman. We have promised to return to them in a few weeks time with some Bibles.... These young men are on fire and keen to go out and preach and teach, but their teaching is limited. They have a great need for study books.... They wanted to know when more SOON people would visit..."

Chapter Seven

TELL THE WORLD

SOON has come a long way since the days when addresses were gathered from telephone directories. Every day letters arrive asking for copies to be sent to friends. Ndria wrote, "I still want to receive *SOON!* to widen and shine my way to our brother Jesus. I hope you will send me more copies of *SOON!* than before, for many pupils in our school. When I tell them about *SOON!* and how it can help people to make their lives better, change them from bad desires and prevent anybody from doing something wrong, they want to receive it so as to improve theirs too and widen and light up their faith in Jesus Christ." So many people have requested multiple copies for distribution in their locality that numbers have to be rationed.

Although demand outstrips the supply, the team is constantly seeking opportunities to break new ground in telling the world the good news of Jesus Christ. Aware that they are God's stewards, they have never embarked on expensive mass publicity. Every avenue of approach is carefully and prayerfully considered.

In 1985, Ad-Evangelism was started with the aim of reaching countries where response to *SOON!* has been smaller. This work is headed up by Tony Whittaker who is responsible for promoting *SOON!* overseas. Tony's first task is to obtain information about newspapers with a wide circulation in the countries to be targeted. Then he has the choice of submitting a small advertisement or writing to the letters page. Writing a letter to the editor is an effective means of advertising the broadsheet as well as being cheap. It stresses both the benefits to those learning English and the fact that *SOON!* can help people find an answer to life's problems.

Sometimes it is even possible to place advertisements in the popular press of countries where Christian activities are normally restricted. An advert in a major Turkish daily brought 200 replies, whilst a total of 1,200 letters were received as a result of two separate advertisements in Indian papers. In February 1991, two newspapers in Ulan Bator, capital of Mongolia, gave a free mention of *SOON!* Some 500 people responded. In view of the significance of this country, everyone who wrote in was offered a copy of *Adventures in English*, an English teaching book based on John's Gospel.

A twenty-year-old student at the Technical University in Ulan Bator was among those who expressed interest. "I understand that you want to help people who are alone, and to introduce them with the life of another people. Also you want to help for studying English. I think it's a good and useful work for us Mongolian readers. There are many English language beginners in my country, but they have not enough materials to read."

For decades Eastern Europe lay under the domination of atheistic despots. Only a few people had the opportunity to hear the Christian message of life and hope. Then, unexpectedly, an unseen arm swept across the nations demolishing physical and political barriers. Almost overnight, the scene changed dramatically and the doors to freedom, locked and barred for so long, creaked open on rusty hinges. Bewildered by this abrupt turn of events, people searched for direction. Many Westerners rushed to proffer material aid. Yet, after enduring years of oppression, the greatest void existed within the human heart. All the wealth in the world could not buy what they needed most – Christ.

At last God's time had come for the gospel to be preached throughout the whole continent of Europe. SOON seized the initiative and very quickly adverts appeared in formerly staunch Marxist periodicals. When God works, things begin to happen. The steady trickle of responses became a torrent. About 4,000 responded to a 'letter to the editor' in the Hungarian *Esti Hirlap*. Over

2,000 replies were received as a result of a letter in *AHOJ* in former Czechoslovakia. When it was mentioned in the post-revolution paper *Romania Libera*, over 1,000 replies indicated the people's obvious desire to broaden their outlook and discover the truth about God.

Albania, one of the last strongholds of communism in Eastern Europe, yielded a record response with over 16,000 letters. These came as a result of an advert placed in *Zeri i Popullit*, Albania's largest daily paper. It is hardly surprising that one reader wrote: "Almost everyone who speaks English is reading *SOON!*" Visitors to Albania reported seeing *SOON!* used in schools, and children memorising passages from *Adventures in English*.

Enkeleda Janku is a young Albanian. Like many others, his letter revealed a real spiritual hunger: "Please help me to learn your wonderful language and to learn more about God. I am happy that you sent me a cassette of *SOON!* and not a book for learning English. They enjoy me very much and I thank you from the bottom of my heart. Also I want that you send me a Bible in Albanian language, over ten copies of *SOON!* because copies of *SOON!* that you sent me, I gave away, and lot of friends after my conversation with them would like *SOON!*"

Targeting educational establishments has produced a

good response from students eager to improve their skills in English. Many express their appreciation for the broadsheets. A professor of English at the West Bank University in Israel wrote to say that he had read the advertisement about *SOON!* in *Al Quds* Arabic newspaper. He believed that *SOON!* would provide a lot of stimulating and interesting material for himself and his students. He said, "I will be very grateful if you kindly send me *SOON!* at my home address on a regular basis."

Word of mouth is always an effective method of advertising and carries with it a personal recommendation. Readers are encouraged to submit names of friends or teachers of English who would like to be placed on the mailing list. This is particularly helpful in areas where other forms of advertising cannot be employed. Incentives, in the shape of foreign stamps or copies of *Adventures in English*, have been the means of obtaining addresses of interested people in countries where response has been low.

Some years ago, SOON 'radio flashes' were prepared for use as fillers between programmes on Christian radio stations. Lasting from 30-60 seconds, each flash had a brief, relevant theme and offered free copies of *SOON!* The object was to reach the millions of non-Christians who listen to these stations. Although this 'marriage' between radio and broadsheets seemed ideal, few radio stations at that time used the flashes, so their effectiveness was limited. However, since the demise of communism, an increasing number of stations, including some secular ones in the former Yugoslavia, have shown interest in using SOON radio flashes.

Promoting *SOON!* worldwide may result in a bulging mail sack for the postman in Willington, but success in the spiritual realm can never be judged numerically. Spiritual birth and continued growth may be difficult to assess. God alone knows the hearts of mankind. In a world of confusing theories and erroneous teachings, many seek the truth, like the Brahmin girl who wrote, "I read *SOON!* and felt some change in myself. I did not understand what 'talking to God' means. Actually I believe in Jesus very much. I like him a lot but I don't know the detail life story of him. I like our god also. I believe in Raghauendra. I feel his and Jesus's life aim was same. Is there any wrong in loving and believing two gods of different castes? I don't think so. If it is wrong please tell it to me."

A law student in India also writes of his desire to know more. "I am studying at Mudurai Law College. I received *SOON!* as a gift copy from my friend.... I want God to change me. I am a nominal Christian. I know that I am a sinner and living in a sinful manner, but I could not get away from that life. I think *SOON!* will help me get more acquainted with Christ. I would like to introduce Christ to my friends also."

Although most copies of the broadsheet are sent abroad, some are used in this country among ethnic groups and in prisons. Stan Leader is responsible for overseeing the prison ministry. The simple nature of the Bible courses makes them particularly suited to those who have no previous knowledge of the Bible. In Birmingham, a retired missionary uses the SOON courses in conjunction with her English class for Chinese ladies. They have also been used to share the gospel with Vietnamese boat people, many of whom subsequently trusted the Lord. Broadsheets and Bible courses even proved a useful means of learning English by people at a Tibetan hill farm in Wales.

Chapter Eight

BE A MISSIONARY FROM YOUR HOME

"It is better to get ten people to do one man's work than for one man to do the work of ten men." This principle has undoubtedly been a key to the successful operation and expansion of the SOON ministry. At the outset, God directed John's attention to the many Christians with reserves of time and energy which could be employed in furthering the work of His kingdom. Utilising manpower in this way has been described as a masterstroke, both administratively and financially. Now, thousands of Christians regularly devote part of their spare time in a collective effort to communicate the love of Christ. They are rewarded, not in any material way but in the assurance that someone, somewhere, will be delivered from the darkness of sin.

With a well-orchestrated system in operation three million *SOON!* broadsheets can be dispatched swiftly and efficiently each year. Geoff McEvansoneya organises the distribution of *SOON!* to Despatch Units and regional distributors. Four times a year Tony Whittaker makes a trip to Worthing to collect the 750,000 broadsheets from the Christian Publicity Organisation. On the way back he drops off bulk supplies to a number of regional distributors. Other regional distributors receive their supplies direct from Willington. The nationwide network of voluntary regional distributors then divide their supplies and transport them to over 1,000 Despatch Units.

The Despatch Units receive address labels which have

been prepared by about sixty typists. Typing addresses at home is a task which demands much patience. The ability to read and interpret illegible handwriting is a greater asset than the ability to type at speed. Unfamiliar place names have sent many a typist scurrying for an atlas in an attempt to locate the town in question. Addresses in Iszkaszentgyorgy and Kiskunfelegyhaz may be familiar to nationals, but typing them when the writing is indistinct is a real challenge.

Although the work may be frustrating or tedious at times, weariness evaporates when the workers hear of the joy that comes when people read *SOON!*, but with broadsheets to the African and Indian continents taking up to twelve weeks to reach their destination, it can be several months before the effect of a particular issue is felt. "We enjoyed *SOON!* very much," one Russian family wrote. "It has already become our newspaper. Through this newspaper you unite people all over the world. You help people to understand what Christianity is."

Although every believer is a full-time disciple, not all are able to offer their services to Christian missions on a full-time basis. Those engaged in the SOON ministry do not face the prospect of learning a new language or having to cope with a different climate. So all Christians, regardless of age, ability, health or home situation, can participate in the broadsheet ministry. One elderly lady, paralysed apart from her hands, testified, "Jesus can use even me."

Moses, Jeremiah and Gideon were all people who felt inadequate for the tasks which God wanted to give to them. They pleaded lack of eloquence, immaturity and insignificance but God overcame their excuses and gave them the strength to do great things for Him. Time has not diminished God's power. He still wants to use ordinary people.

The life of one lady changed abruptly when ill-health forced her into early retirement. The future looked bleak and a long-held desire to serve the Lord seemed mere wishful thinking. Then one day she walked into a Christian bookshop and was handed a copy of the local church magazine. Glancing through the pages, she noticed an item highlighting the need for SOON Bible Course markers. The opportunity to be involved in this literature outreach appealed to her. She quickly applied and before long, a new sphere of Christian service had opened up for her. Like many others, she discovered the joy of pointing others to Christ.

Phyllis Knottley believed God was calling her to a new ministry but, at 69, she wondered what she could do. Opportunities in counselling were not available because she was too old. Time went on and she became more and more frustrated as all the doors shut in her face. Reading one day in Joshua, she was arrested by a note which she had written over chapter five: Gilgal – place of rest, refreshment and redirection. About to visit 'Filey in Skegness', Phyllis wondered if this might be her Gilgal, the place where she would find redirection. On the first morning there, she was reminded that God often calls, reverses and restores. Wondering what God had in store, her excitement mounted.

It was Wednesday before she had a chance to see the missionary exhibition. Looking at the stands, her attention was drawn to the name *SOON!*. Although aware of the ministry, she had dismissed it, thinking it simply involved addressing envelopes. That evening, however, her eyes focused on a single panel marked, 'Answering Problem Letters'. Suddenly everything clicked into place: writing, counselling, sharing her Bible knowledge and practical experience. She could do them all without having to leave her chair!

About a month later, her first batch of letters arrived, accompanied by a bundle of tracts and advice on reading poor handwriting. She was launched on the most worthwhile job she had ever done. To many she has become 'mother'. Sharing the love of Christ with her family of children overseas has brought Phyllis a joy that clearly demonstrates the value of investing in lives for the kingdom of God.

Mary Jones of Islington in London formed the very first SOON Service Corps with two helpers. Today, back in her native Scotland, she continues to despatch copies of *SOON!* on her own. Many others have continued in the ministry for a number of years. They are unsung heroes who wait for that glorious day in heaven when they will embrace those from distant tribes and nations to whom they wrote and for whom they prayed.

Fired with enthusiasm, some churches have adopted a

particular country or area. They not only despatch copies of *SOON!* but also deal with the response and follow-up where necessary. In some cases it has resulted in life-long friendships and visits to the country concerned.

For many former full-time and spare-time helpers, SOON has acted as a launching pad into Christian service both here and abroad. Without the opportunity to serve God in SOON, much valuable gifting would have been wasted.

Prayer is a vital aspect of all Christian ministries. It is the power house: the place where battles are fought and won. SOON has many prayer partners. With the help of the monthly Prayer News and quarterly Prayer Digest, individuals and groups regularly remember the work. The following poem from an early copy of Prayer Digest demonstrates the value of prayer:

Living in the bush, he was miles from anywhere,
Where the missionary seldom came and stayed.
But then the Holy Spirit winged
  a broadsheet over there –
Because you prayed!

He was studying the Bible course 'A Change of Life for
  you';
As he thought about his life, he was dismayed.
But then the Holy Spirit spoke, "The Bible words are true!"
Because you prayed!

He found conflict in his heart.
Should the gods that he had known,
Or should Jesus be the One to be obeyed?
But then the Holy Spirit brought to life
The good seed that was sown –
Because you prayed!

No doubt prayer is the reason why responses have even come from Christmas Island and Tahiti in the Pacific Ocean although no one knows how copies of *SOON!* reached them.

The value of prayer is also seen in the following article where the broadsheet describes itself.

I am a WEC missionary and a very good one too! They say that missionary means 'sent one' and I am really that in every sense of the word. My first language was French and I communicate effectively in all parts of the French-speaking world. Early on, I branched out into simplified English. But I did not stop there – I now speak Portuguese, Spanish, Nepali, Thai, Swahili, Turkish, Arabic, Indonesian, Italian and more recently Romanian. So you see I am quite a linguist! I travel the world and need no visa. A stamp will take me anywhere I wish to go, even into so-called closed lands. I turn up in the most unexpected places. Once I found myself in the wastepaper basket in a Brazilian prison and was used in the conversion of many of the prisoners.

I reach both high and low with the good news of the gospel. My readers may be anything from peasants to presidents, students to seminary professors. Do I get results? Certainly. Thousands have been brought to Christ through the testimonies I contain and some of these enrol for Bible correspondence courses. In some countries, converts group to form Readers Clubs or even churches. This is not to say that I have been entirely without opposition. The devil is no friend of mine and has tried to keep me out of some quarters. However, wherever I go, I am accompanied by the prayers of God's people. That is the secret of my success.

Chapter Nine

WHICH LANGUAGE NEXT?

At one time it was felt that only forty per cent of the world's nations would profit from the use of the English language as a means of spreading the gospel. Now, the success of *SOON!* has proved that the whole world is open to gospel broadsheets in easy English.

SOON! is an excellent way of reaching young people with some knowledge of English, but it is of little use to the older generation who have rarely had the same opportunities to learn English.

Following the success of *Bientôt* and *SOON!*, the potential for gospel broadsheets in other major languages has captured the imagination of a number of Christian workers. While some people have made direct translations of existing broadsheets, others have used the concept as a basis for producing their own literature. Prayer partners and practical helpers are needed for each version. In every venture the aim is to achieve a spiritual harvest. Many obstacles have to be overcome to launch each version and consideration has to be given to the question of financing them.

The Portuguese *Cedo*, used both in Portugal and overseas, was established by Leslie and Bessie Brierley who once worked in Portuguese Guinea (now Guinea-Bissau). When they lived at the British WEC headquarters with Fred Chapman, they were often the target for his light-hearted banter, much of which centred around the launching of new broadsheets! Fred's enthusiasm for this method of spreading the gospel inspired them.

God used Margaret Brown, the former missionary to Pakistan, to launch the Urdu version, *An Quarib*. One day some letters, written in Urdu, arrived at the SOON office. They were in the Arabic script with which Margaret was familiar so she duly translated them. Not long afterwards, John Lewis planted the seed-thought, "Why not produce an Urdu *SOON!*?"

Establishing *An Quarib* took some time because a calligrapher had to be found, as well as Pakistani translators. The process was further complicated by the need to send the material to Pakistan first, so that it could be written out by the calligrapher. Marlin and Barbara Summers, who had relocated to Pakistan after being unable to return to the Indian-Tibetan border, were willing to act as co-ordinators there. When the broadsheet was ready they returned it to Britain for printing.

By the time Margaret had to relinquish her work, Marlin and Barbara were ministering to Asian immigrants in Britain. They willingly accepted responsibility for the broadsheet and for a number of years supervised the production and distribution of around 45,000 copies each issue. Sadly, publication ceased in 1989 for reasons beyond their control. However, it is hoped that in the future it will be possible to start up again.

Another missionary, Margaret Coleman, had worked in Zaire before moving on to Kenya in 1961. Eventually returning to this country, she worked as a staff nurse at Newmarket hospital. In her spare time she began to mark

SOON Bible courses from students in East Africa. As their English was often poor, Margaret sometimes added notes in Swahili. One day a student wrote, "Please send me *SOON!* in Swahili." The need was obvious, but who could produce it? Margaret felt she did not possess the skills for such a task and her husband was well past retiring age. However, during a WEC staff meeting, Margaret was challenged when another missionary, Iain Mackenzie, said that if God calls a person to do something, they should go ahead and do it. Inspired by that remark, she went ahead. In the autumn of 1980 the first tentative issue of 10,000 copies of *Upesi* was printed. Today the circulation averages 80,000.

Grubby, scrappy letters from schoolchildren in Kenya request *Upesi* for themselves and their friends. Swahili being the national language of Tanzania, this country is one of the main target areas, and copies are sent to evangelists and pastors for distribution. Recently, large numbers were requested by one bishop's office for distribution to churches throughout his diocese.

Upesi has also found its way into Mozambique, as many evangelists take copies with them when visiting. Letters tell of those finding deliverance from satanic darkness. "I would like your help with copies for preaching the gospel, for these testimonies, showing how people can be freed from the slavery of Satan, are a great help to many," wrote Rev. Nyembo from Zaire.

Gospel Literature Worldwide continued its expansion. As the need for new language versions was recognised, so God had His servants trained and ready for action. There are broadsheets in Arabic, Indonesian and Spanish. The Thai broadsheet uses a different title for each issue. An English *SOON!,* similar to the main one, has for some time been produced in Australia, targeting particular countries in the Far East.

A recent arrival is *Presto,* a four-page leaflet in Italian. The first issue, distributed in all parts of Italy with the aid of local helpers, was well received, with a considerable number of people writing in for the Bible Course. Although costly, the leaflet is being produced for Albania as well as Italy.

In Eastern Europe, too, many of the older generation have little or no knowledge of English. The opening up of this area revealed people with a desperate desire to discover the true meaning of life. Indoctrinated for years, they found it difficult to distinguish truth from error. The time was ripe for God's Word to be made available to feed many hungry hearts.

Curind!, the Romanian *SOON!,* was the first to be translated and distributed on a large scale. Two churches in Britain who were burdened for Romania sponsored the first edition. The demand was so great that a further 20,000 copies had to be printed. Thousands of Gospels have been given out in that country since the revolution. The spiritual need is even greater than the need for food and medicines.

As *perestroika* and *glasnost* swept through Russia, Christians there became concerned about the spiritual needs of their fellow men. Valdemar Kalinin, a gypsy poet belonging to the Russian Baptist Church, was able to produce a pilot edition of a Russian *SOON!* at the end of 1991.

Volker and Susan Schmidt, who served for three years as full-time members of the SOON team, now produce a small magazine in easy German entitled *Der Weg* (The Way). The magazine, which started regular production in September 1992, is aimed at the wide-open doors of Eastern Europe. The Schmidts are well aware that nobody knows how long the present freedom will last.

"I got your magazine for the first time," a reader from Russia wrote, "and I was greatly impressed by it. I didn't realise that something so interesting existed. I could not tear myself away from its pages. Everything is of great interest. Thank you very much for it. It is especially good that you send your issues free of charge. Our high prices don't even allow many of us to buy the press of our country, not to speak about any foreign papers. You bring us much joy. I hope to receive the next issue of *Der Weg* soon." A reader in Bulgaria wrote, "Your magazine gives me hope that our life will be better. It shows us our way in life and our purpose for living."

SOON has also made inroads into Nepal, the world's only Hindu kingdom, where changing one's religion or encouraging others to do so has been a serious criminal offence. In 1977 teachers of English in all 550 high schools were contacted and an incredible ten per cent responded. By the mid 1980s, Ian and Jean Mackevoy, who handle this area of the SOON ministry, were in regular contact with several Nepalis. One of these, a man named Shashidhar, submitted a complete, handwritten translation of *SOON!*. In an accompanying letter he stated that

God had given him the vision for a Nepali version and enquired about the possibility of publication. He was encouraged to proceed with printing in Kathmandu.

Shashidar holding the Nepali broadsheet

The first issue of *Chandai* was presented to Ian and Jean on their visit to Nepal in February 1989. There they had the joy of meeting Bishnu, another keen, fearless believer who also had a vision for a Nepali *SOON!!* The two men formed a team. Bishnu is responsible for the printing, distribution and follow-up of *Chandai*. Shashidhar, with his wholehearted dedication to the Lord, excellent English and understanding of local culture and Scriptural truths, is ideally suited to the task of translating and editing the broadsheet.

Each broadsheet is different, tailored to meet the needs of a particular group of people, but all share a common aim – to attract attention and communicate the good news of Jesus Christ in a way that is easy to understand.

Chapter Ten

VISION FOR THE FUTURE

"Into all the world," were the Lord's instructions. So it has been SOON's aim over the past thirty years to gain admittance to all countries regardless of their political or religious status. Governments opposed to the gospel have made this task difficult at times. But where God is concerned, no country or individual is beyond the reach of His love. Radio and literature have both been ways of sharing the good news with those in countries where the missionary is barred. No curtain, iron or bamboo, has ever proved totally impenetrable. Although care is needed, people are being reached and the remarkable church growth in many so-called closed lands bears witness to this.

The following letter from Morocco demonstrates the obvious spiritual hunger that exists in those parts of the world dominated by Islam. "I would be so glad if you could help me by giving me some information and answers to my questions. Really I do not know what to do. I want to be a Christian, but how? What should I do? What should I believe in? I want to find a new way in my life. Could you help me please?"

Today, the teaching of English has become a major

missionary opportunity. Even in countries where human liberties are restricted, students and teachers alike appreciate help with learning English. With few educational aids available, any material is welcome.

"Being a student I want to tell you that *SOON!* is very helpful to my learning English," writes Bing from Shanghai. "Thank you for giving me such good reading materials. I am interested in these significant stories and I read it more and more. At first my reading level wasn't well in my class. The English teachers told me to find some English articles to read. Later I was discouraged because those articles were too difficult for me. Just then, fortunately, I received *SOON!*. I found it not only improve my English but also give me a lot of knowledge about God. Before long, my English teachers and classmates asked me in surprise, 'How could you make a great progress in English?' So I introduced *SOON!* to them and I gave them the other two pieces of *SOON!*. After having read, they also felt *SOON!* is useful for learning English well."

Ability to communicate in another language demands skill in speaking as well as in reading and writing. Always quick to take advantage of appropriate modern technology, SOON commenced a cassette ministry in 1985. In the beginning spare-time helpers from all over the country read articles from *SOON!* on to cassettes, adding a brief, personal message if desired. However, a wide variety of British accents was not always helpful to *SOON!* readers abroad! So now the master-tapes are produced by a special team.

Cassettes are carefully packed by Marie Hopkins. Sometimes they are wrapped in metal foil to prevent erasure when screened at custom points. Occasionally toilet paper is used as padding so the cassettes will not be detected. One recipient expressed his thanks for the toilet paper, not having seen any for years! The cassette, however, was never mentioned!

A young Polish woman listened to a recording of *SOON!* and wrote for some Bible helps. When the sender posted a New Testament and book of Bible stories she included a packet of needles and thread. The young woman was especially delighted because it arrived on her twenty-first birthday.

Learning a new language is exciting and SOON cassettes are an innovative approach to language learning. Students pay attention to what is said because the cassettes contain true stories which are full of vitality. At the same time they are being exposed to the light of the gospel and the possibility of salvation.

From the middle school in Shangdong, China, a teacher wrote, "Thank you for recording the articles for me. I enjoy your voice very much. It is so clear I can hear every word. It'll surely give me much help in my English studying and teaching. Once I played it to my students, they said they could hear some words although only beginners. I think it not only gives me help in my English studying and teaching but also helps me to understand what the life means. I like the article 'I made them famous.'... It told me what the real happiness is."

Recently English teachers and students in China and Mongolia have been supplied with copies of *Adventures in English* (based on John's Gospel) in addition to cassettes. In this way the strongholds of the evil one are being pierced by the sword of the Spirit.

The following letter from China illustrates the need there: "I have received *SOON!* through the help of my colleagues.... Although I have never believed in God in my life, I think what the stories in *SOON!* talk about is really true. I have done many wrong doings in the first thirty years of my life.... By reading *SOON!* I am sure I can throw away the wrong selfish desires and will enjoy the real freedom and joy from Jesus Christ.... Now I am not a Christian but I want to be in future. I need a Christian's Holy Book,... and SOON Bible Course by post."

Exploring other avenues of approach into closed areas led SOON to implement a pen-pal scheme. Correspondence with a pen friend helps to build bridges of friendship. This in turn may provide opportunity for sharing the gospel. In view of the great demand for pen friends, the scheme has to be limited to countries where other forms of Christian outreach may be restricted. For many years communist countries in Eastern Europe were the main source of requests. Today requests from China and the Middle East receive priority.

To avoid possible complications it is not normal practice to link members of the opposite sex. The majority of requests coming in are from young men, some of whom are quite unashamedly looking for a girl friend. In Middle Eastern countries, where a young man may have to pay a high price for his bride, an English girl might be seen as a bargain! So there is a great need for more young men in Britain to become pen friends.

Well-established friendships have often resulted in visits, strengthening the bond already created through letter writing. One correspondent spent a year teaching English in China where he had the opportunity to meet his pen friend. Much to his delight, his friend later trusted the Lord and then led others to Christ.

Man-made political and religious barriers have proved no match for the glorious gospel of Jesus Christ. "Though I am a Muslim," wrote a twenty-seven-year-old from Turkey, "I always believed in Holy Bible of Jesus Christ but very unfortunately I have not been directed through any sources towards Jesus Christ and his commandments, not sufficient literature available. Nowadays I am serving sentence of couple of years and got ample time to study about Christianity. I really need peace of mind and beg you to furnish me with all opportunity and facilities."

In thirty years *SOON!* and the other broadsheets have, in the goodness of God, made tremendous strides. Such is the power of the love of Christ that satanic strongholds around the world are crumbling and the great commission is being fulfilled. *SOON!* knows no boundaries.

At the beginning of the decade the team formulated a five-year expansion plan. They are already exploiting the opportunities presented by new freedom in the former communist countries. They would also like to see SOON operating on a much larger scale in China. Then there is the vast potential of the under-evangelised Muslim world.

The team's goal is to produce one million copies per issue. CPO share their vision and are ready to handle the increased workload. To make this goal a reality will require a further 500 Despatch Units and more full-time workers. With a higher distribution rate worldwide, more students will embark on the Bible Courses. So by 1995, a total of 400 Bible Course markers will be needed.

The vision is not limited to broadsheets. John Lewis is always alert to new opportunities to advance the work. Further initiatives being developed include radio programmes and textbooks for teaching English, easy-to-read books on science and the Bible, and the use of videos.

One of the reasons for SOON's success is that people all over the world are eager to learn English. Radio Worldwide are producing an English-by-Radio series using *SOON!* material and augmenting it. This combination of radio and literature could be an effective way of spreading the gospel.

The collapse of communism means that students and teachers of English in many countries are desperate for good textbooks. The literature section of TEAR Fund gave a grant to SOON to enable them to send packs of *Faith in Action* books to English teachers in these countries. Each pack contains one copy only of each book, but it is hoped to make cassette recordings of the books, enabling whole classes to listen to the stories, hearing good English pronunciation.

The books, in easy English, include the stories of David Wilkerson, Nicky Cruz, Jackie Pullinger, Gladys Aylward, Dr Barnardo, William Booth, Elizabeth Fry, John Dodd, Corrie ten Boom and Sadhu Sundar Singh. They cover highly relevant issues such as poverty, drug addiction, homeless children, rehabilitating prisoners and anti-semitism. The biographies show how Christians can be instrumental in remedying these problems.

Under atheistic communism the theory of evolution was used to discredit belief in God. Now that communism itself has been discredited, many university teachers seem to be disillusioned with this theory and are ready to consider the idea of creation. Therefore, the possibility of sending easy-to-read English materials on the relationship between the Bible and scientific subjects, such as creation and evolution, is being explored.

Videos are now used extensively in Africa and Asia. The *Jesus* film has been shown widely throughout Africa, and many have responded to Christ as a result. Few people in the Third World can boast much in the way of material benefits, but televisions and video shops are a fairly common sight. The demand for videos is on the increase. Peter Hopkins, who joined the SOON team in 1992, hopes to exploit this effective means of communication in gospel outreach.

John Lewis has devoted his life to fulfilling the goal of WEC: to bring back the Lord Jesus Christ as King as quickly as possible, by a definite attempt to reach the unreached peoples of the earth in accordance with Matthew 24:14. This was also the goal of C.T. Studd, WEC's founder. A famous all-round test cricketer from a wealthy family, he turned his back to fame and fortune to spend the rest of his life as a missionary in China, India and finally Africa, where he died. When challenged about the sacrifices he was making, he answered, "If Jesus Christ be God and died for me, then no sacrifice can be too great for me to make for Him."

John Lewis is convinced that we must use all the modern media which God has put at our disposal. *SOON!* is an effective, attention-getting means by which this is being achieved. But much remains to be done.

Today, perhaps as never before in the history of missions, God needs you. The SOON job centre is always open and can guarantee to find work for all.

Requirements:

Age: Immaterial

State of health: unimportant

Previous experience: not essential

Qualifications: divine motivation, faith, perseverance. Ability to type, paste, mark, write or pray.

Hours of work: One or two evenings a week/month/quarter depending on the nature of the job.

Salary: Luke 6:38. Joyful fulfilment and a reward in heaven assured.

Appendix

Gospel broadsheets available at the time of publication:

Bientôt (French): Unit 6, Garcia Trading Estate, Canterbury Road, Worthing, W.Sussex, BN13 1AL, England.

Cedo (Portuguese): Apartado 2294, 4700 Braga Codex, Portugal.

CP 1005, 3240 970 Contagem, Minas Gerais, Brazil.

Chandai (Nepali): PO Box 5382, Kathmandu, Nepal.

Der Weg (German): Andoverstr.77, 47574 Goch, Germany.

Presto (Italian): Casellá Postale 314, 00125 ROMA-ACILIA, Italy.

SOON!: Vere Lodge, 44 Twyford Road, Willington, Derby, DE65 6BN, England.

PO Box 1292, East Victoria Park, WA 6101, Australia.

Upesi (Swahili): 81 Rozel Court, Beck Row, Bury St. Edmunds, Suffolk, IP28 8AY, England.

Ven (Spanish): Apartado 49.023, 28020 Madrid, Spain.